Healing The Wound

The Family's Journey Through Chemical Dependency

Mathias Karayan

Healing The Wound

The Family's Journey Through Chemical Dependency

Cover: Oil Pastels by Maria Monterey; aprés

Library of Congress Control Number:
2006905925

ISBN-13: 978-0-615-13226-6

Contents . . . .

Forward

I have been privileged to work with Matt Karayan for many years. I have seen Matt combine his life experiences of over 20 years and education in the field of chemical dependency, to help chemically dependent people and their family members.

Matt is very creative, a master of spontaneous therapy. His empathy is unquestionable. Happily, for care-givers as well as those of you in need of help in this area personally, Matt has developed a curriculum for educating people which he clearly shares in this book.

This education has helped hundreds of families who came to Matt feeling helpless and hopeless. They have been surprised as you will be, by how Matt interjects his sense of humor into his education. Daily, I hear how he has touched many families as he has touched my own life.

After many years of work in this field, I believe this book will help those of you who will not have the opportunity to have contact with Matt. His wisdom and love for people has encouraged many, as this book can help you.

Joan Giorgio MA, LADC
Director of Treatment Services of New Beginnings, Waverly
6/06

Dedication:

To My Father Edward Kuntscher,
who taught me forgiveness

Introduction

There is a place where a path stops at the bank of a river. Near this place sat a scorpion, patiently waiting for a ride across the river. A fox, wandering along the bank, came to the place where the scorpion waited. The fox carefully surveyed the bank for a way to cross, but did not notice the scorpion. Finally, the scorpion spoke: "Good day, Mr. Fox!"

Startled, the fox jumped back from the bank. "Oh my!" apologized the scorpion soothingly. "I mean you no harm. It's just that I've been waiting here a long time for a way to cross this river, and I fear that I may not be able to find my love. Could you help me with a ride across?"

"But I know who you are," said the fox. "I have heard that your sting, though numbing at first, causes nothing but pain."

"That is true," said the scorpion sadly. "Those who have been unaware of me have had that experience. That seems to be my affliction. But I can see," continued the scorpion with admiration, "that *you* are wise, true to your word, and quite capable of taking care of yourself."

Taken in by the scorpion's charm, the fox did not turn away, but continued to listen. "And so it is," appealed the scorpion, "that I ask for your cooperation. We both are looking for a way to cross this river. You can swim to the other side, but I cannot. However, on your back—and of course because of your help—I can see over the waves to the best access on the other side. This partnership could help both of us reach our destination. And you would really be doing me a great favor."

With one last waver of doubt, the fox protested: "You could sting me, and I could die."

"I recognize your concerns," said the scorpion ingratiatingly, "but if I were to sting you, you would drown, causing me to die as well. Of course, I'm putting myself at risk as well, since you could end our partnership whenever you choose."

Finally convinced by the scorpion's reasoning, the fox committed himself to the partnership. With the fox's consent, the scorpion climbed on, and the fox walked down to the water. As the fox swam into the current, the scorpion called out directions. The scorpion felt light on the fox's back.

Just as the scorpion had said, the fox could not see over the waves. (However, the fox did not realize that he could not see his way because the scorpion's weight on his back pushed him lower in the water.) And so he continued along as the scorpion navigated.

Occasionally, the fox would wonder aloud why the crossing seemed to be taking longer than it should. But then the scorpion would either assure him that they were almost there or express hurt because the fox doubted him. The fox, not wanting to offend, struggled on through the ever-changing current.

The cold water gradually numbed the fox's senses and kept him unaware of his growing exhaustion and loss of direction. Also, the weight of the scorpion pressed steadily downward on his back. The fox entertained thoughts of giving the scorpion up to the current. But how dare he think such a thing? How could he turn on a friend who needed him, a friend who had been trying to help him across this river? And besides, the fox thought: "I gave my word."

As the fox became exhausted and totally vulnerable, the scorpion suddenly stung him. "Why are you doing this?" asked the confused fox with one last gasp of air. "Now we both will drown!"

"I couldn't help it," answered the scorpion. "It's my nature to kill." [1]

The allegory above, borrowed and adapted from the storytelling traditions of native peoples, illustrates the tricky nature of addictive chemicals, such as alcohol, marijuana, crack/cocaine, methamphetamine/speed, and others. But it also reflects the dangers of becoming too entangled in the life of a chemically dependent person.

This book is written for those closest to—and therefore most affected by—a chemically dependent person. Although we will spend some time discussing our chemically dependent loved ones, the primary focus of this book is not on understanding *them*. Our focus throughout this book will be on understanding *ourselves*, the affected loved ones, who have developed a preoccupation with them (the chemically dependent) and in doing so, have adjusted our lifestyle around their preoccupation with their chemical. By examining our thoughts and behaviors, identifying what our preoccupation looks like, and determining why our preoccupation persists, we will be able to come to a crossroads that allows us to look at different choices. These choices will open new doors for an honest renewal of hope for our recovery. Do not think this is a selfish choice—that thought only breeds guilt. It is our guilt (out of fear) that prevents us from understanding the forces that have brought us to this situation in the first place. Only an honest look at other options can help us develop a blueprint for a healthy future.

A Voice for Different Choices

Our preoccupation has been to want to help, to want to rescue our chemically dependent loved ones from self-inflicted harm. However, nothing we have done has stopped their persistent journeys towards self-destruction. In fact, some of the things we do *contribute* to this destruction.

This dilemma will be addressed, along with the question "Can I exercise unconditional love while allowing my loved one to suffer?"

There *is* hope for all of us who suffer. But to access that hope, we must be open to a voice that is different from the ones to which we have been responding. It is a voice that speaks of different choices that will lead us in a new direction. It is for us to develop the habit of listening for this voice, a voice that was always there, but has been drowned out by our preoccupation with our chemically dependent loved ones. Learning to listen to this voice reminds us of our own journey, the one we have forgotten because of our preoccupation. (We will learn more about listening to the voice of a Higher Power [2] in Chapter 4).

This is not a book about drug identification and its effects. That topic is addressed in other books. However, no matter what mood-altering chemical/drug of choice we are talking about, we encounter:

1) a common cluster of symptoms,

2) a predictable progression,

3) an inevitable outcome if the progression is not interrupted, and

4) the effects and reflections of the above items on the family.

This book's goal is to help individuals understand how a powerful preoccupation (such as a mood-altering chemical) can change a person's life. While the first three areas listed above will be addressed primarily in the first chapter and indirectly in later chapters, we will focus more heavily on how a family member's drug use affects and is reflected by the rest of the family. Therefore, this book is written primarily to help *you*, the family member, clarify how *your* powerful preoccupation has affected *your* life. With this clarification, you will find renewed hope and personal strength joining you on your journey. These two friends will help you once again hear the voice for different choices; choices that lead us all back to peace of mind.

Chapter 1

Whose fault is it?

Whose fault is it?

Within your blueprint, you become the choices you practice

The Big Book of Alcoholics Anonymous (AA) describes alcohol as "cunning, baffling, powerful!" [3] Actually, all mood-altering chemicals can be described this way. Addictive chemicals are **cunning** because chemically dependent people think they can control their use or safely use their chemicals of choice without becoming addicted. Users cannot see the implications of how their drug use can unravel their lives. Addictive chemicals are **baffling** because while users think they are controlling their use or can get their use under control, their economic, financial, social, personal, family and spiritual lives are, in fact, unraveling towards self-destruction. Addictive chemicals are **powerful** because not only can users not control them nor admit the need to quit, but also because the chemicals are driving their life decisions in the direction of self-destruction.

A Common Cluster of Symptoms

What are the symptoms that indicate a person's use of mood-altering chemicals has become more powerful than his or her will?

- Using more of a drug at a time than he or she intended;
- Increased frequency of use;
- Manipulative behavior;
- Lying;
- Defiance;
- Missing family events;

- Isolation from family and friends;
- Decreased attention to personal hygiene;
- Exchanging sober friends for friends who use mood-altering chemicals themselves;
- Changes in social activities;
- Dropping out of recreational activities;
- Problems with school and work;
- Blaming others for mistakes and problems;
- Attempting to control and/or hide his or her drug use;
- Legal problems.

In addition to the above symptoms, methamphetamine addiction is a fast-progressing addiction that in its third stage of use (High Intensity Use) includes symptoms of:

- Disturbed sleep habits that involve being up for a number of days and nights and then crashing for long periods of time, to be followed with being up again for a number of days and nights. This is what is called the meth cycle;
- An inability to sleep that produces sensory deprivation resulting in paranoia, panic, delusions and aggression;
- A change in eating patterns (not eating) which involves severe weight loss;
- Repetitive behavior and/or restless uncontrolled movement, tremors;
- Open sores, facial scabs, rotten teeth;
- Memory loss;
- Depression;
- Stroke;
- Heart failure.

It really is cunning. Did you see all of this coming? If you are telling yourself: "I should have seen the signs," you are still underestimating the cunning nature of the drug.

It really is baffling. All of your guilt and anger comes from your inability to understand what is happening right under your nose.

It really is powerful, more powerful than you. In spite of all your attempts to stop the addiction, the addiction has prevailed. It is the reason that your loved one has changed before your eyes.

A Predictable Progression and an Inevitable Outcome

Invariably, we ask ourselves these questions:

• *In spite of all the drug education, why did they try it?* They tried it out of curiosity.

• *Why do they continue to do it?* They continue because they like what it does to them.

• *Why can't they stop?* They can't stop because they do not want to believe that what they like (and come to love) is a destructive force that is more powerful than they are. This is what denial looks like.

• *Why don't they want to see the obvious: that it is destroying them?* They do not want to see the obvious because they do not want to grieve the loss of what they have come to love more than anything else.

• *How do we know they love it more than anything else?* How else can we explain their self-destructive preoccupation?

• *Why do they blame us, their parents/family members, for their use?* If they can believe that the way they were raised and/or their current living conditions have something to do with their addiction, they can believe that the problem has to do with something outside of them. What they are really doing is attempting to bargain with their powerful preoccupation in order to avoid dealing with the fact that the problem is within them.

• *What will happen if our child/loved one continues to use mood-altering chemicals?* With continued use, the inevitable outcome is institutions, jails and death. The means by which chemically dependent people reach these results is through insanity. As Albert Einstein said: "Insanity [is] doing the same thing over and over again and expecting different results." Insanity's partner in crime is denial—"a lie to oneself" that denies the facts that they cannot control this powerful preoccupation and that they cannot avoid the inevitable outcome. Linked to this is their denial or resistance to seeing that they really love their chemicals more than anything else, and their refusal to even see the inevitable outcome of their continued drug use.

• *What will happen if we don't acknowledge that mood-altering chemicals are more powerful than any of us?* You will continue to employ guilt and blame to punish your loved one—and yourself.

The Endless Search to Nowhere

Guilt, blame and anger only serve as roadblocks to understanding chemical dependency. When family members feel guilty because they believe that they should have seen the problem, they often try to make things "right" by taking such actions as paying the addict's bills and/or getting them legal advice to avoid consequences. They don't understand that addicts use this kind of help to further their addictions. Our attempts to help just continue an endless cycle of addiction—worry—assistance—addiction.

So we see that a mental search for the cause of a loved one's addiction is endlessly fraught with worry, embarrassment, shame, guilt, and ultimately, frustration. When you embark on this type of search, you will never find resolution, because the reason for your loved one's chemical dependency is somewhere else. Again, simply stated, people become chemically dependent because they like how the chemicals affect them. And they like the effect so much that they don't want to believe this effect is more powerful than they are (and so are in denial).

Guardians and parents too often look at the symptoms of excess drug or alcohol use and think: "They lie, cheat, steal, and blow off family rules, including curfew. They are not doing well in school or on the job. They've even been kicked out or fired. They're not learning what they need to be an independent adult. They're not taking on responsibilities like the other kids their age. Where did I go wrong?"

It is tempting for parents in particular to judge their effectiveness *as* parents by looking at outcomes. And the parent who has had the good fortune of raising an "easy" child contributes to the problem. "Let me tell you how to raise your child," they say. "Look how well mine have turned out. I can tell you what you did wrong." You may or may not have done anything wrong (as you perceive it). But contrary to conventional wisdom, what you may or may not have done is not relevant. What is relevant is that your child behaves the way he or she does because of the influence of a cunning, baffling and powerful preoccupation with mood-altering chemicals.

Our Minds: Friend or Foe?

The most powerful tool we possess is our minds. When we suggest that our minds look for something, our minds will search until they find it. It just may not appear in the form we ask. So when we ask, "Did we do something wrong?" we are asking our minds to seek out only information that will bear witness to that particular question.

Your mind always finds
the witnesses you ask it to find

Selective hindsight finds thoughts like this: "Maybe I was too strict. Maybe I was too permissive. Maybe I should not have married someone who turned out to be an alcoholic. Maybe I should not have gotten divorced. Maybe I wasn't around enough to nurture. Maybe I gave him too much of my time. Maybe it's because I am or have been actively chemically dependent and a bad role model. Maybe I should have seen it sooner so we could have gotten the proper help early on. Maybe as a sibling or friend, I should not have introduced it to him or should not have used with him or gotten the chemical for him." The lists go on and on, while the guilt builds and builds...without resolution.

The fact is that you are collecting distortions through the eyes of guilt. Your loved one has a will of his or her own. The perceived mistakes you have collected through your ruthless investigation have **no** cause-and-effect correlation except through your own assumptions. You can only "suppose"—and never know for sure—that what you did in the past had anything to do with this person's addiction. Your cause-and-effect correlations can only be hypothetical guesses.

Why do you ask the same self-accusing questions over and over again?
Because your guilt seeks resolution.

Why are the self-accusing questions you ask never resolved?
Because they are questions that have no answer.

Why do you ask questions that have no answer?
Because your guilt seeks resolution.

If you had done things differently, would life have been different for the chemically dependent family member? You can never know for sure, because the question is hypothetical. And even though you can never know for sure, guilt asks the same self-punishing questions over and over again. The only thing you accomplish with this analysis is to destroy your peace of mind now.

Guilt's stranglehold on you serves no purpose except to punish yourself for something you did not do. This blocks your ability to see other reasons for your loved one's problems.

Your ruthless investigation only complicates the process of healing.

The First of Three C's

Al-Anon, the supportive organization for family members of alcoholics, has a list of three "C's" to help individuals understand the limits of their responsibility: cause, control and cure. The first of the three "C's" states: "You did not **cause** it!" When guilt incites you to think that your actions caused a chemically dependent family member to behave the way he or she does, ask yourself this: Can you honestly say you worked hard to model lying, stealing, cheating, etc.? Of course not. Some of you may say: "But I did lie, steal, cheat, etc. I was also active in my chemical dependency." In that case, there is no denying the fact that you may have missed opportunities to demonstrate healthy modeling. But many successfully adjusted kids have come out of traumatically dysfunctional households. As adults, they attest to the fact that these experiences made them strong. To them, these difficulties were simply challenges they rose above.

Do you deny the idea that challenges and failures make you a better person? Every reason you give for why your loved one is chemically dependent because of your mistakes, I can give as a reason why another person is successful in life.

No Respect for Boundaries

Chemical dependency pays no attention to boundaries. It affects the rich, the middle class, and the poor. It shows up in small families and large families. It touches nurturing, bonded families as well as dysfunctional, fragmented families. No ethnic heritage escapes the plague of chemical dependency. What, then, does have an effect on the presence of a chemically dependent member of a family? Social learning? Genetics? Parenting skills? Life experiences? In the next few paragraphs, we'll address what effect differences in these areas have on chemical dependency.

Social learning

Social learning does not explain the differences among children from within the same family. The idea that an ever-expanding/adjusting family structure will raise different children does not explain parents' early recognition of a child's inherited predisposition. Though some inclinations toward impulsivity, sensitivity, moodiness, etc. can be modified by social conditioning, parents see differences of temperament in their children before social learning has a part to play.

The dynamics of social learning cannot be denied. However, where one child might take too much for granted or feel entitled because of everything given to him, another child might learn stewardship or selfless generosity. Where one child might fear authority from being raised in fear, another may become that fearful authority—or learn to teach love. One child might hold onto issues of resentment and act them out because of perceived events in the past, while another learns the power of forgiveness because of those events. Attempting to explain the nature of these differences does little to identify why one person becomes chemically dependent and another does not.

Genetics

However, some studies suggest that *heredity* does influence one's response to mood-altering drugs. These studies do help us better understand the baffling nature of chemical dependency. For example, one study has found that "identical twins born to alcoholic parents are more likely to become alcoholic than fraternal twins born to alcoholic parents. (Identical twins share identical genes; fraternal twins do not.) And, adopted children of alcoholic parents show higher rates of alcoholism than children of non-alcoholic parents. This is true even when children of alcoholics are raised by non-alcoholic foster parents."[4]

While this information should not be used to minimize the effect that parents have on their children or to diminish their responsibility to direct their children, it does offer another reason for parents who have racked their brains trying to do "the right thing" for their kid, only to seemingly fail in their efforts.

Parenting skills

Some children are manipulative, deceptive and defiant. As parents, we also note certain tendencies of dependence, independence, sensitivity, impulsivity, perfectionism, etc. among our children from early on. It becomes our task to encourage their strengths and teach them to work with, temper, or extinguish what we see as self-defeating characteristics. Sometimes the child's temperament is beyond our skills as a parent to change, and help is required. Is asking for help a sign that you have failed? Or is it a sign that you have come up against something more powerful than your skills as a parent?

You may have done all the things necessary for the raising of your child. Even so, you were not there when someone invited your child to try a mood-altering drug. And the fact that some children are more prone to abusing mood-altering chemicals than others in the same family attests to a disposition of biological vulnerability. When it comes to being fair in raising your children, sameness cannot be the measure. No two kids in any family are the same. Fairness involves the flexibility to work with the strengths and weaknesses that each child's blueprint brings into the world.

Life experiences

Your loved one did not start using drugs or alcohol to escape some "unresolved traumatic event" out of his or her past. People try mood-altering chemicals simply out of curiosity and/or peer pressure. Once addicted, they seize the idea of "escape" as a way to justify their actions, to assign blame, and to deny that they have an addiction more powerful than they are. As long as addicts can believe their problems have a cause outside of themselves, they think they can bargain with the problem and learn to "use" socially. Acknowledging that the problem is within themselves means admitting that they are vulnerable to a mood-altering preoccupation more powerful than they are—and recognizing that they will have to give it up. The idea of letting go of something that they have adjusted their whole lives around can appear fearfully unbearable.

Parents, family members, I am not trying to exonerate you. But your preoccupation with trying to absolve yourself from guilt and blame by focusing in on them has become a self-defeating part of the problem. Just like the addict, acknowledging that the problem is within yourself means admitting that you are vulnerable to a preoccupation more powerful than yourself— and recognizing that you will have to give up this preoccupation. And the idea of giving up something you have adjusted your whole life around can appear fearfully unbearable.

If you want to pride yourself on the idea that you are more powerful than every power over your loved one, then accept the guilt for how you have failed them.

However, if you acknowledge that there are powers greater than you (and there are), then you can let go of the guilt and move on to make other choices on how to deal with your chemically dependent loved one.

Exercise:

List all the things you think you should have or should not have done to make a difference in whether your family member became chemically dependent. Also, list all the people, places and things you tend to blame for your loved one's chemical affliction.

_____

_____

_____

_____

_____

_____

_____

_____

WHOSE FAULT IS IT?

When you have completed your list, ask yourself: "Can I ever know for sure that things would have been different if I would have done this differently or seen it sooner?"

When you finally come to the conclusion that you can never know for sure, then you can see how you have misdirected your thoughts and energy. You have been asking questions that have no answers. The only thing you find is a propensity to beat yourself up over and over again. Your attack on yourself through guilt is not helping the situation. Not only does it make you feel obligated to rescue the chemically dependent person, but more importantly, it also destroys your opportunity for peace of mind now. Only when you are at peace with yourself, can you become aware of a different set of choices and have the energy to make choices that will be part of the solution.

In the light of a cunning, baffling and powerful adversary, no matter how this particular person was raised, someone was going to come along and say to them, "Here, try this." And your family member would have. Do you know why they would have? Because they did!

Out of guilt and shame, you have victimized yourself. Out of blame, you have tried to victimize others. This is your time to begin to free yourself by identifying and interrupting self-accusing thoughts.

Chapter 2

The Family's Insanity

The Family's Insanity

"But I don't want to go among the mad people,"
Alice remarked.

"Oh, you can't help that," said the Cat: "we're all
mad here. I'm mad. You're mad."

Lewis Carroll
Alice in Wonderland

Preoccupation

In the beginning of my educational sessions, I ask
family members to set goals focused on themselves.

I ask that their goals relate to *their* journey, with
their personal issues, to be something for *them* to
work on, and to be actions that they can take within
the realm of the current session's work. However, the
most common goals I hear stated by family members
are either "I want to support them" or "I want to
understand them so I can help them."

I also hear numerous other comments, usually
focused on the chemically dependent person. Because
family members have lost their focus on themselves,
they pick goals that focus on others. This kind of goal-
setting always results in frustration, *because the
goals are not within their power to achieve.*

It is true that chemically dependent people put
themselves through a lot of pain. It is *not* true that
they suffer more than the loved ones who worry
about them. In fact, and arguably, the family members closest to the chemically dependent person suffer *more,* because they do not use a numbing device
(the mood-altering chemical) to escape from or forget
their dilemmas. (However, that is not to say that family members close to the chemically dependent person

do not make attempts to avoid, escape and/or deny their dilemma in ways that we will talk about later in this chapter.)

Family members' attempts to change a chemically dependent loved one are valiant. They are also futile. Even though their efforts are in vain, they try, try and try again in the hope that something different will happen. This futility proves not only the cunning, baffling and powerful nature of chemical dependency, but also is a witness to an insanity the family does not understand.

Remember:

> *Insanity is doing the same thing over and over again, while expecting (or hoping for) different results.*

Though the changes in a chemically dependent person's lifestyle due to his or her preoccupation with drugs are not always evident to him or her, they are obvious to family members. However, the lifestyle changes that family members experience because of their preoccupation with a chemically dependent loved one are not always so obvious. It is even less obvious to the family members that their own preoccupation is not helpful to the chemically dependent person. And just like the chemically dependent person who tries to hide or justify his or her preoccupation, family members also try to hide or justify their preoccupations. In the same way, both behaviors become self-destructive.

As parents, family members or friends, we watch chemically dependent loved ones struggle, and we feel an obligation to help them. Maybe, we think, just a nudge will help them get on their feet. Caring for them unravels into repeated rescue attempts, finally becoming a preoccupation of worry, guilt, anger and despair. It really is cunning. It tricked us. As our attempts to help turn into exercises of frustration and anger, our response often becomes a numbed "I don't care what you do!" In worn-out despair, we state: "I've tried everything I can. I don't know what else to do." It really is baffling. It does not make sense. And even now, we feel guilty about our response to them when at first we just wanted to help them over the hump. "What happened?" we cry in confusion. We have met a power greater than our attempts to help.

Justified Support?

Before we can understand what it really means to help a chemically dependent person, it is important to understand the affliction. The best way to understand the affliction is to understand how we ourselves have been afflicted. We can start by understanding what support is not, by honestly questioning ourselves about our ineffective help and by then closely examining our typical justifications for it:

Have I believed them over and over again without any change in their behavior?
"But this time they might mean it. I need to be available to help in case they mean it this time!"

Have I kept secrets from my spouse, other family members and friends?
"I don't want them to look bad; I want them to have good relationships!"
And, *"I don't want to look bad. I'll be embarrassed."*
And, *"I promised them I wouldn't tell. If I did tell, I'd be a 'snitch' and they would get mad at me. Then I might lose my relationship with them and my ability to help them."*

Have I lied for them to their boss?
"I don't want them to lose their job; this is their life . . . and my financial security!"

Have I lied to their school?
"If I can just get them to graduate . . . then I can let go!"

Have I bailed them out of jail?
"Yeah, but they might learn how to be a criminal or get hurt by a criminal!"

Have I driven them around?
"I have to, or they will drive drunk and kill themselves and/or someone else. Besides, how will they be able to take care of their business without a license? And how will they get to their support meetings?"

Do I pay their bills?
"I don't want them to have bad credit, or lose their home, or go bankrupt. They'll just dig a deeper hole!"

Do I make their appointments and call to cancel when they fail to show up?
"I don't want them to look bad." And just maybe, *"I don't want to look bad!"*

Do I give them money for rent, bills, food, clothing, gasoline, etc.?
"I can't have them living under a bridge, they will die!"

Do I become a messenger for them between other family members?
"They need help mending communication problems!"

Do I avoid, become numb, or tolerant of their disrespectful behaviors?

"If I lower my expectations, maybe we can come to a workable compromise!"

Do I walk on eggshells around them to save the peace?

"If I say the wrong thing, they might explode and/or go out and drink!"

Do I make excuses for them?

"Their boss really is a jerk!" or *"They really are misunderstood,"* or *"The loss of a loved one really hit them hard!"*

If we assume that their preoccupation with their chemical of choice is the number-one resident within the "kingdom" of cunning, baffling and powerful, then none of our actions has or will help them stay sober. In fact, when they are preoccupied with getting their chemicals, they will twist whatever we do to help into a means of getting their drugs. What we call "support" has actually enabled their drug-using lifestyle. As a matter of fact, without our help, their fragile world would have a difficult time existing.

Enabling behaviors are the actions we take in an attempt to help them overcome a particular situation. Actively-using chemically dependent people take that help and twist it to support their drug-using lifestyle. Our insanity is doing it over and over again expecting and eventually hoping for different results. This cycle is insane because the help we offer actually contributes to and helps prolong their affliction.

Support Gone Sour

It is understandable that you want to protect your loved ones from harm. But do you realize that your attempts to protect them often set them up for continued exposure to harm? Consider the following scenarios created from the patterns we see in real life.

Susan lets her son live with her so he is safe from the world. The result? His ability to overdose in Susan's home becomes an easier and more comfortable opportunity than somewhere "out there," and he turns her home into his drug den. Susan justifies her decision by saying "At least I know where he is."

Tammy does not have gas money to get to work because she spent it on her chemical-using lifestyle. So when she asks her sister Rita for gas money, Rita gives it to her, hoping Tammy will be responsible this time. The result? Thanks to Rita's help, Tammy now has the gas and money to drive to the dealer and buy drugs. When Rita confronts her on it, Tammy first lies about not having a job. Pushed further, she screams: "I didn't use it *all* for drugs!"

Bob thinks he has finally wised up and can out-manipulate the manipulator. He knows better than to give his brother money. Joe will just spend it on alcohol. So Bob buys and puts food in Joe's refrigerator, pays Joe's car insurance, and puts gas in Joe's car (a car Bob has to keep making payments on, so he doesn't lose his part of the investment that Joe has defaulted on). The result? Now Joe can drive the car to the bar and liquor store, where he pays for his alcohol with the money he hasn't had to spend on groceries or gas.

Marge argues angrily with her daughter, who no longer listens to her "nag." Marge feels she's done everything she could. From trying to love her daughter into sobriety to a feeble attempt at "tough love,"

Marge says: "You name it, I've tried it; it doesn't work!" Of course these methods didn't work, because Marge has only *tried* them. She's *tried* lots of things, hasn't been consistent with following through on any of them, and nothing has changed. No wonder she's confused, angry and hurt.

The above examples of enabling behaviors are by no means exhaustive, but they remind us of how our best intentions are twisted by chemically dependent people to support their using lifestyles.

If you honestly admit it, you see that nothing you have tried has kept your chemically dependent loved one safe from harm. In fact, he or she has continued to be out of control. Earlier, we looked at Al-Anon's first of the three "C's": You did not cause it!" Now we will examine the second of the three "C's": "You cannot **control** it!"

Your loved one has not been changed by your attempts to help. All your enabling, manipulating, bargaining behaviors testify to the fact that you cannot change him or her. You persist with all your enabling, manipulating, bargaining behaviors because you don't want to believe that you cannot in some way change him or her. And even though the chemically dependent person (in his or her own unconscious way) continues to teach you what is not yours to control, you continue in the insanity. Why?

Because I Love Them: A Mask for Fear

It is easy to accuse chemically dependent people of dishonesty. Their very lifestyles demonstrate it. However, it is time for us to be honest with ourselves.

When I ask: "Why do we persist with the insanity of enabling chemically dependent people, when it is clear that our attempts to help actually contribute to the continuation of their illness?" the most common answer I hear is: "Because we love them." I do not deny that you love them, but enabling behaviors have nothing to do with love. There is another feeling that the above list has in common and it is one we try hard to avoid: *Fear*.

It is true that you want to protect your chemically dependent loved ones from harm, relationship/family loss, bankruptcy, loss of home, employment/educational issues, legal issues, the shame of failure, etc., but your need to protect them masks the real reason behind your preoccupation.

Your preoccupation with them helps you avoid the fact that you have not been acting out of love. Instead, you have been reacting out of fear.

Earlier we looked at guilt and embarrassment as powerful motivators in placing blame and responsibility where they do not belong. But fear is an even more powerful motivator that feeds guilt and denies us the ability to make sane choices on behalf of our loved ones.

You are afraid. You are afraid of your own shame and embarrassment; afraid of losing a relationship with them; afraid they might not think you love them; afraid they might not love you; afraid they might go to jail. You are afraid they might die. But most of all, and least focused on, is your fear that you might have to experience your own grief and pain of seeing them go through their own grief and pain. And you don't want to face the fear that there is nothing you can do to protect them from it.

And so it is that your chemically dependent loved one is held hostage to a powerful preoccupation: a mood-altering chemical. You yourself are entangled with your own powerful preoccupation: your afflicted loved one. But through your denial, you are held hostage by your own fear.

The good news is: This you can change, because it belongs to you. Remember, the only goals that are within your power to achieve are those that focus on yourself.

You have encountered something more powerful than you, and it is not your fault. Your own list of enabling behaviors is witness to how hard you work to avoid, deny, and escape this fact. Your denial of this fact results in fear, anger, guilt and sorrow because the outcome is not yours to control. In short, the actions you have been justifying in the name of love, you have been doing out of fear.

Said another way, nothing you do will prevent them from learning the lessons they are destined to learn. Accepting this is to come to the place of real hope, not fear. Here is where we start healing the wounds caused by chemical dependency. We'll be exploring this more deeply in Chapter 4.

The Cycle of Insanity

Your cycle is this: The basis of your relationship is love. Your attempts to help redirect the chemically dependent person to healthier living have been attempts to help him or her avoid consequences that you fear. Yet your repeated attempts to protect him or her from the consequences that you fear have only enabled him or her to continue with self-defeating behaviors. It has made it easier for your chemically dependent loved one to continue with and even escalate the very lifestyle that provokes fear in you. And in fearful reaction to watching him or her escalate towards self-destruction, you again try to out-maneuver and manipulate him or her to produce outcomes you think or hope will help.

The fact of the matter is that your reactions out of fear in an attempt to protect them has allowed their powerful preoccupation to continue much more easily than if you were not around to "help." Your fearful attempts to protect them have actually contributed to their physical and mental deterioration. Insanity (doing the same thing over and over again, while hoping for different results) reigns.

Consequences: The Best Teachers

Consequences are the "best teachers" because consequences "interrupt" the chemically dependent lifestyle. However, out of your fear of what those consequences might be, you have actually been working hard to protect your chemically dependent loved one from his or her best teachers. Your protective, enabling behavior has cultivated an environment that feeds the drug-using lifestyle. In turn, the potential for consequences continues and escalates. The enabling actions you have taken in hopes of avoiding fearful possibilities have only provided continuing opportunities for fearful possibilities.

> *"How do you know I'm mad?" said Alice.*
> *"You must be" said the Cat, "or you wouldn't have come here."*
>
> Lewis Carroll
> Alice In Wonderland

Denial is necessary for this unhealthy pattern to continue. Through their own denial, chemically dependent people do what their drug dictates, not what they might truly want to do. They are also in denial as to the seriousness of their addictions and their consequences. You, their family members, are also in denial. Your denial is about how much you avoid confronting the ways in which fear has blocked your ability to choose sanely. Not only do you want to avoid the fact that your feeble attempts to redirect, control and out-manipulate them has failed to protect them from what they want to do, but you also want to avoid the fact that you really cannot protect them.

Exercise:

All your attempts to help have been used by your chemically dependent loved one to support his or her drug lifestyle. Not only does this reveal the power of this preoccupation, it also reveals how you have adjusted to and responded with behaviors that actually feed his or her addiction (enabling behaviors).

Given this definition, list examples of your enabling behaviors that have supported the lifestyle of your chemically dependent loved one. Be specific.

_____

_____

_____

_____

_____

_____

_____

_____

_____

_____

_____

_____

_____

_____

If insanity is doing the same thing over and over again while expecting different results, then enabling is surely insane, because the results have been the same. Your chemically dependent loved one has not changed. In fact, he or she has gotten worse.

Recognize why you enable this behavior. It is not because of love. Your love is a given. Your list of enabling behaviors has one thing in common, and it is fear. Yes, you love him or her, but your current relationship is based on fear. When you are willing to identify your enabling behaviors for what they really are, then you can begin the next step of your journey.

You can't change them, but changing the way you interact with them breaks the cycle.

An Arena of Different Choices

By recognizing that you cannot change chemically dependent people, you step into an arena of different choices. Remember, the old arena was fraught with arguing, frustration and fear. Your shift means you are no longer focused on trying to change them. Instead, your renewed focus is on changing the way you interact with them. You are empowered now because *this* is something you can change.

Knowing what support *is not* helps you learn what support *is*. Support is *not* trying once again to help the chemically dependent person in your old fearful way. To learn what support truly *is*, you must move past your fears. Walking through your valley of fear will bring you to new choices for supporting your chemically dependent loved one; choices other than the same old fearful reactions, choices you never saw before, but were always there. You couldn't see them because you looked through the eyes of fear, a fear that distorts the view.

Because fear results from a lack of information, you yourself will need to accept help and support. In upcoming chapters, you will be shown a path that provides you with direction, one day at a time, one step at a time, through your valley of fear. And, as you will learn, you do not walk this path alone.

Chapter 3

Who are you?

Who are you?

In our attempts to change them, we change

We have talked about parental guilt in the light of cunning, baffling and powerful chemicals. We have also talked about how we may deny that our relationships with chemically dependent loved ones are based on reactions made out of fear, and how this denial is hidden under the guise of "because I love you, I need to rescue you." Very cunning indeed. The baffling part is that our attempts to protect our chemically dependent loved ones from harmful consequences has only helped prolong their misery as well as our own. The chemically dependent person's desire to repeat and maintain this baffling scenario is so overpowering that through our attempts to change them, we change.

We have also mentioned that "interruptions" (such as saying "no' and sticking to it) have consequences that interfere with the drug-using lifestyle. In this chapter, we will look more specifically at how we can change the way we interact with our chemically dependent loved ones through such "supportive" interruptions. But first, we must look at how our denial, fear-based reactions and enabling behavior have changed us, rather than them.

How Have We Changed?

Chemically dependent people can be argumentative and coercive. We too become verbally aggressive and argumentative when we react to their behavior. In fact, many of us have become "nags" who are increasingly tuned out. Think about your arguments. If your conversations weren't ridiculous in the first place, they quickly became so. Chemically dependent people argue about stupid things. We engage in those stupid conversations with them.

Chemically dependent people may avoid reality or confrontation. Over time, we too avoid facing reality, or perhaps we just become numb to our chemically dependent loved ones' words and behavior. We also may isolate ourselves by avoiding certain people so that we don't have to lie or feel embarrassed. We walk on eggshells around the chemically dependent person to "save the peace." (What peace? Walking on eggshells is very tense!) Maybe we don't want to say the wrong thing, so they don't get upset and go out and use drugs.

Just like our chemically dependent loved ones, we lack balance. Either we are "nags," or we avoid speaking our truth. Have we become so emotionally tied up with the chemically dependent that we don't know how to act or respond in natural ways?

Chemically dependent people violate their integrity by lying, compromising work ethics, verbally abusing loved ones, and not being true to their word. We violate our own integrity by keeping secrets, lying to them and for them, compromising responsibilities to ourselves and others, being verbally abusive out of anger, feeling guilty for our own abusive behavior, making threats/bargains and not following through. It's been too easy to focus on how we can't rely on them to follow through with what they say. Is it also true that they can't rely on us to follow through with what we say? "

Chemically dependent people try to manipulate us so that they can continue their drug use. In the previous chapter, we looked at a list of enabling behaviors we use with the chemically dependent people in our lives. Do you realize that these enabling behaviors are actually our attempts to out manipulate them into changing?

Chemically dependent people become more tolerant of their chemicals, needing more of them more often, to get the feeling they seek. So too do we become more tolerant of the behavior of chemically dependent people, compromising our values, compromising the safety of our homes and families, allowing ourselves to be verbally and physically abused, and reaching numbness without ever touching a mood-altering chemical.

Chemically dependent people ride an emotional roller coaster. And so do we, when we allow the insanity to take us from hope through rage to despair.

Chemically dependent people blame whoever or whatever for their circumstances and justify their actions because of it. We preach at them about needing to take responsibility for their lives. "It's your bed, you made it, and you will have to sleep in it!" we scream. And yet, how easy it is to blame the chemically dependent for the ways in which *they* have messed up not only their lives, but our lives as well. Do we also have our own slippery slope of denial about our own responsibility?

Avoiding Responsibility

We are angry with them because...why? You say: "Because of what they are doing to their lives, as well as the chaos they are causing in mine!"

You've heard the saying "Fool me once, shame on you. Fool me twice, shame on me." But I am not talking about you believing them the second time. I am talking about you believing them the hundredth time.

I am not saying there have not been times that your chemically dependent loved one has not spoken to you with honest remorse and a desire to change. They have! And you believed them—once again. It's easy to want to believe them when they are speaking in a moment of honest vulnerability. But then, the next moment...there they go...running off to the dope dealer. Now you feel angry, taken for a chump... again. And you were.

You have failed to realize once again what addicts continually fail to realize. Their addiction has power over their choices. So why are you mad at them? Did your chemically dependent loved one make you step into the boxing ring to get sucker-punched for the hundredth time? How many times does it take for you to wise up before you stop loaning money with no return in finances or lifestyle change? Either you are a chump, or you are in a situation that is over your head...let us say, beyond your power.

Chemically dependent people invite chemicals into their lives over and over again, and they look for someone to blame. You allow yourself to invite their misery into your life over and over again and then blame and punish them for the misery you invited into your life. You argue that the chemically dependent person needs to take responsibility for his life while you refuse to do it yourself.

Chemically dependent people are not good at setting boundaries and keeping within them. Neither are you. They compile lists of resentments. You also collect resentments and air them on a regular basis without resolution. Have you become like the chemically dependent person, an angry nag that argues, picks, and punishes?

Through our "justified" anger, we always attack. But we are not aware that when we attack, we always attack ourselves first. We attack ourselves first because when we are angry we cannot have peace of mind. I am not saying that anger is bad or wrong. In fact, anger can be productive if it causes in us a fundamental shift that breaks us out of the cycle of insanity. But our anger can be destructive when we repeatedly vent or lash out, feel remorse, apologize and then continue back in the cycle. If we do not change the way we interact with our chemically dependent loved ones, we will again set ourselves up to feel used and abused by them. Because our interactions do not have a resolution, they are added to our arsenal for the next time we feel used and abused—another piece of weaponry to be hurled at a chemically dependent family member as a reminder of what a "loser" he or she is.

Through anger held on to over time (resentment)
We keep an ugly past alive in the present
by playing it over and over again.

Your chemically dependent loved one does not make you ride his or her emotional roller coaster between hope and despair. You chose to ride. He or she did not make you believe the one hundredth lie. You chose to believe it.

Recognizing the Cause of Anger

We can deal with anger when we take responsibility for being the cause of our own frustration. While bodies can clash, and words can seem cruel, you have the power to decide what that clash and those words mean to you! In other words, *you* decide what effect you will allow any person, event or thing to have on you. In the final analysis, you recognize that you are reacting to your own interpretation of your life events. This recognition empowers you to accept that:

You can change your reaction
by changing your view.

If you perceive an emotional reaction as "*you* making *me* angry," you become the victim of your denial, because it is not another person who makes you angry. It is your interpretation of another person's actions that makes you angry. And if it is your interpretation of life events that can enslave you or free you, you can choose differently. You can choose only those interpretations of life events that witness to your freedom.

Remember:

We cannot change chemically dependent people, but by changing our view of what events really mean, we will change the way we interact with them.

Honesty allows us to see that we are mad at our chemically dependent loved ones because we have not taken care of ourselves. We need to acknowledge that our unwillingness to follow through with self-care is not another person's fault, nor is it their problem. Just like a chemically dependent person's situation is neither your fault nor your problem, it's not his fault that you have decided to make his problem into your problem!

And so we encounter Al-Anon's third "C": "You cannot **cure** it." And if you do not believe this, you will try to save that which is not yours to save and end up punishing your chemically dependent loved one out of your own restless discontent.

The Issue of Setting Boundaries

The issue is not setting boundaries to keep the insanity out. You have been very good at establishing many boundaries many times. It is the "many boundaries many times" that demonstrate your problem. They are witnesses to the fact that you have not been good at *following through* with the guidelines you establish. The chemically dependent person is inconsistent. So are you.

Listed below are 15 lies we cherish to justify our enabling behaviors. Not only do these lies maintain our denial of how powerful the addiction is, they also sabotage our ability to maintain healthy and consistent boundaries. They also keep us from identifying fear as our primary motivation for our insane behaviors.

1) It is within my power to change you.

   Truth: *Your enabling behaviors have demonstrated otherwise.*

2) It is up to me to help you avoid pain.

   Truth: *It is for each of us to learn through our own pain. What I can learn from you, I can accept when I am ready to learn it. Pain is a part of living but my suffering is optional.*

3) I protect you because I love you.

   Truth: *Honestly, you try to protect me out of fear.*

4) I am in charge of how you, my child, interpret your life situations.

   Truth: *When I threw a temper tantrum as a two-year-old because I did not get what I wanted, did you teach me to do that?*

5) I am responsible for your self-esteem.

   Truth: *Many children who come out of disadvantaged families have used those experiences to build their characters and be successful. Many children who have come out of nurturing families do not like who they are. Explain this?*

6) My child should have every advantage or I've handicapped them.

   Truth: *We all take life on its own terms and make it be for us what we want it to be.*

7) Fighting/conflict in the family means I am not a good parent.

   Truth: *Because conflict is the reality of this world, it is the means we use to teach us to rise above.*

8) I cannot say "no" because you might not think I love you.

   Truth: *You cannot say no because you fear the loss of a relationship you already do not have. Stop competing with a chemical. I love my chemical first and foremost. And besides, it is not for the parents to try and have their needs met through their child. This just confuses everything!*

9) My child needs me to be a friend.

> Truth: *I already have friends, many of them misguided. What I need is direction.*

10) My rescuing behaviors keep you safe from harm.

> Truth: *Of course this is a lie. None of your enabling behaviors have kept me from using my chemicals. I have been out of control. Do you really think you have been able to keep me safe from harm?*

11) If I do not rescue you, I am abandoning you.

> Truth: *Stop attacking yourself with guilt. You can't abandon me, because I have already abandoned the family/relationship for something else. And it really isn't a matter of me abandoning you as much as it is a demonstration of a cunning, baffling and powerful chemical taking over.*

12) When I rescue you, my life is easier.

> Truth: *For a moment you have relief, but the problem comes back over and over again. You are far from free.*

13) I can love you into sobriety.

> Truth: *Yes, love is the answer, but it will never force its way through a closed door. I am numb and oblivious to whatever your attempts are. I will use whatever you give me to feed my addiction.*

14) If only you liked yourself.

> Truth: *It is not a problem of poor self-esteem. Many people with poor self-images are not chemically dependent. Many people who are all about themselves are chemically dependent.*

15) If I make it easy for you, it might help you stay sober.

> Truth: *It doesn't matter how easy or difficult you make it for me. If I want sobriety more than anything else, I will find it.*

These lies have one thing in common, and it is not love. It's fear!

No Time for Guilt

This is not a time for guilt. This book is about clarification so you can move through guilt. We have enabled others out of fear. With clarification, we can make different decisions.

We have believed our chemically dependent loved ones over and over again because when they promised us the sun, the moon and the stars, we so badly wanted to believe them. Then the next minute, they were out chasing after their drug dealer. Yes, we have been duped. So have they. Their inability to stop their use merely proves the power of their addiction. They are in denial of this. So are we.

Our attempts to change them without results are not proof of our failure.

They are the proof that their addiction is more powerful than us.

When you are told by the addict, "You don't understand my struggle," he or she is right. Just don't be taken in by this excuse, because addicts don't understand the power of their addictions either. If they did, they would not be in the mess they're in.

When the chemically dependent person says: "I know that what I was doing was wrong, but I couldn't help it," how is that different from your attempts to avoid, escape and deny the insanity that unraveled in your life, before your own eyes?

When you are told that you cannot relate to his or her pain and suffering, that is also a lie. You have suffered the worry of staying awake many sleepless nights (without a numbing agent), wondering if you will get a phone call saying your chemically dependent loved one is dead. Have we not been conditioned to experience fear merely by the sound of the telephone and, in an insane way, feel relief when we hear that a loved one is "safe" in jail?

Who Are You?

Who are you? What have you become? What are your passions? What are your worries and cares beyond your fears for the chemically dependent person? Through your preoccupation, you have forgotten about you. It is time to refocus. This is not a selfish endeavor. It is understanding that you must first be healthy yourself before you can be of help to anyone else. You have not done this very well.

The emotional roller coaster you ride is not yours. It belongs to the chemically dependent person. You were not forced to get on. So get off!

Exercise:

Changing what you have become involves an honest inventory to identify what it is you have become. If you look closely, without blame and guilt, you will find that your thoughts and behaviors are a reflection of the insanity surrounding your chemically dependent loved one. Don't be afraid to look. You want to look at these behaviors so you can change them.

On separate pieces of paper, list each way you have changed while attempting to change your chemically dependent family member. In your own way and time, burn the parts of that list you are ready to change.

You can't change what you deny.
You can only fear its existence.

We, like our chemically dependent family members, have gotten lost in the dark valley of "cunning, baffling and powerful." Through this preoccupation, we have forgotten about the power that we are. It is time to remember.

Chapter 4

The Language of
Letting Go

The Language of Letting Go

You must be the change you wish to see in the world

Mahatma Gandhi

In Chapter One we discussed how changes to our chemically dependent loved ones occurred because the chemicals that they took eventually took them. Addictive chemicals truly are cunning, baffling and powerful. You learned that the guilt of what you "should" or "should not" have done is irrelevant because of a curiosity to experience something new and the addiction itself that are more powerful than you. Chapters Two and Three pointed out that in your fearful attempts to change a chemically dependent family member, you changed. Through your attempts to save the chemically dependent person from getting lost, you have lost your way. It is tempting, at this point, to argue: "Why do I have to change? It's the addict who messed up!" Remember, you are the one caught up in your own cycle of insanity and in need of a new path.

Why Do They Relapse?

One of the demons that haunt chemically dependent people is the "patiently waiting" desire to alter their moods. This demon whispers: "Go ahead, take a hit or have a drink; you're in control," or "Just one more time, for old times' sake. No one will know." While it may seem that this cunning aspect of addictive behavior is what causes a relapse, it is not the real reason. Lack of personal honesty is the key.

The Big Book of Alcoholic Anonymous explains it best. "Rarely have we seen a person fail who has thoroughly followed our path. Those who do not recover are people who cannot or will not completely give themselves to this simple program, usually men and women who are constitutionally incapable of being honest with themselves."[5]

The paradox is,

When we are honest about our limitations, we are free.

Do you still think you can make chemically dependent people be honest with themselves? Your enabling behaviors and nagging sermons tell you "no." The old adage "You can lead the horse to water" (and you have, many times), "but you can't make him drink," rings true. In fact, at times you may have wanted to drown him in your trough of truth simply out of frustration.

More importantly, can you honestly say you have been honest with yourself? If you really want to support your chemically dependent loved one, this will be the place to start. Are you ready?

What is Support?

Without all of our fearfully preoccupying, self-defeating distortions getting in the way, we can now talk about what the word "support" really means. Support starts when we learn what it means to take care of ourselves first. How do you save someone from drowning when you yourself are drowning right next to them?

A parent once told me of a dream she had about her chemically dependent child. In it, her child was drowning. The parent desperately wanted to save her child from a watery death and quickly leaped into the water. When she reached her child, the panicked child latched onto the parent and tried to use her as a ladder to reach the surface of the water. The parent desperately treaded water, but every time she tried to get a breath of air, the child pushed her head under the water. The parent soon realized that in her efforts to save her child, she herself was going to drown. Fear seized her. How could she leave her child, just to save herself? But if she didn't leave her child to struggle for survival on his own, she too would die. And if she remained indecisively frozen with fear, both would certainly drown. Before the dilemma could be resolved, the parent woke from her dream in a cold sweat.

Taking care of ourselves first means:

- allowing our chemically dependent loved ones to sit in jail until morning rather than lose a night's sleep by picking them up at 3 a.m.

- paying our own bills first rather than getting behind on the rent because we paid our chemically dependent family members' gas/electric/phone bill.

- being honest with our friends about our loved ones' chemical dependency, rather than lying to them so that they don't think badly of our family.

- letting our chemically dependent family members miss work rather than being chronically late ourselves because they frequently oversleep, miss the bus and need a ride.

- refusing to experience the stress of acting as a messenger between our chemically dependent family member and individuals with whom they are fighting.

- saying what we believe rather than keeping our opinions to ourselves because we're afraid our chemically dependent family members will disagree.

- expecting our chemically dependent loved ones to live by the same standards as the rest of us, rather than making excuses for their behavior.

- ending all the enabling behaviors that diminish us and do nothing to end the suffering of our loved ones' chemically dependent lifestyle.

The argument "Supporting them helps me" hides your excessive willingness to deceive yourself into leaving your own fear unresolved. Others will say "I will do whatever it takes," deceptively and recklessly concealing their true feelings, which are: "As long as 'whatever it takes' does not make me deal with my own fearful reactions." To do "whatever it takes" is to make the decision to first begin to work through your fearful preoccupation. It takes honesty.

"How can I support them?" you ask. The first and foremost step for support will be your willingness to be honest with yourself. Read on.

Let Go of What?

We mentioned earlier that if a chemical addiction were not interrupted, the results would be "institutions, jails and finally death." This is a chemically dependent person's journey through their insanity. "How can I let go of my loved one in the light of this?" you fearfully cry.

When I ask family members: "What control do you have over the chemically dependent person that you need to let go of?" most look bewildered, struggling for an answer. Some say "my enabling behavior." We have the power to give up our enabling behavior only because it is our own behavior. But this does not answer the question, because it does not address the issue of control. Again, I ask: "What *control* do you have over the chemically dependent person that you need to let go of?" Some say "fear." We do have the power to give up our fear because it is ours, but our fear has had no effect on controlling them, so that is not the answer either.

The July 26 entry on AlAnon's Courage to Change: One Day at a Time daily reader reads: "I'm learning to identify illusions that make my life unmanageable. For example, I wanted to stop controlling people and situations, but the harder I tried, the more I felt as if I were knocking my head against a wall. Then someone mentioned that I couldn't give up something I didn't have. Perhaps I could try giving up the illusion of control. Once I saw that my attempts to exercise power were based on illusions, it was easier to 'Let go and let God.' "[6]

The truth is that we can't let go of control over a chemically dependent person—because we do not have control over him or her. It would be like telling you to "give up control of the wind." Would you respond by saying, "I'm trying to, but it's hard to do"? How ridiculous and crazy that would sound! And yet that's what we think when faced with the decision to give up our control over a chemically dependent loved one.

We can, however, give up the *illusion* of control, because that is all it is. If you think about it deeply, we have an *illusion* of giving something up, because we can't give up what we don't have. Said another way, you can give your loved one up because you never had them in the first place.

God grant me the serenity
To accept the things I cannot change
The courage to change the things I can
And the wisdom to know the difference.
Reinhold Niebuhr

At this point, some people are hit by the panicky feeling of entering a void of doubt. Then the light of recognition dawns. "You mean that all my attempts to control were based on illusion?" The miracle that releases you whispers calmly, "Yes." This is your opportunity to step beyond denial into freedom.

By becoming more honest with ourselves,
we don't just say the Serenity Prayer; we live it.

Denial and control are like walls of a jail cell that we've built around our hearts. Once we accept that the cell walls are just an illusion, we realize that we've always been free to trust a Higher Power. Faith in a power greater than ourselves reminds us there is a plan greater than our little attempts to control our little distortions of fear. A parent once asked me to pray with her to place her chemically dependent loved one in the hands of God. I told the parent that I'd rather pray with her for reassurances that she herself is already in the hands of God, and for help in using these reassurances to remember that her chemically loved one is also *already* in the hands of God. All of our prayers to put our chemically dependent loved one in the hands of God were not for them. Those prayers were for us. When we remember that we are already in the hands of God, we will remember that our chemically dependent loved one is already there too.

In Psalm 23:4, David the shepherd needs to walk through his valley of the shadow of death. It is time for us to pull up our tent stakes and walk through our valley. David reminds himself: "I fear no evil; for Thou art with me; Thy rod and Thy staff, they comfort me" (New American Standard Bible). We have avoided for so long the relationship of trust that our Higher Power waits for us to have. There is no fear in this place. Just rest.

What Relationship?

Through your attempts to protect, you have been trying to hold on to your relationship with your chemically dependent loved one. You are now being asked to let go of that relationship.

You might be surprised to find that the idea of letting go of the relationship with your chemically dependent loved one generates feelings of anger and fear inside you. Suddenly you're realizing how much you've invested in this relationship. This relationship has left you feeling guilty and angry for being used. You've worried about abandoning your chemically dependent loved one, but now you're recognizing that he or she abandoned you to worship a chemical. You might suddenly recall all the times your chemically dependent loved one lied, cheated and stole from you. Memories come flooding back of all of the times that he or she promised the moon and the stars and presented you with heartaches and tears instead. Your anger is understandable, but it's time to remember that your loved one did not abandon this relationship. Instead, his or her actions merely demonstrate the power that the mood-altering chemical(s) have over his or her life, over his or her power to choose.

It's now time to realize that you don't really want

the relationship you are being asked to release. The truth helps us see that the awareness of our relationship of love has been blocked by reactions made out of fear. You want to let go of this so you can learn detachment with love. In the light of truth, this is not hard to do because this is what you want to do.

Grieving as Part of the Process

From another perspective, we can understand our chemically dependent loved ones' behavior if we see them as going through a process of grief. Just the thought of giving up their chemicals can initiate this grief process in them. Not only are they in the process of grieving the loss of a loved one that they never possessed in the first place (their chemicals possessed them), they are also in the process of grieving the loss of a lifestyle that they totally adjusted to their addiction.

The chemically dependent person's process of grief involves the following elements: denial ("It's not hurting me" or "It's not that bad"), bargaining "I can control it" or "It's your fault"), anger ("It's not fair; why can you use and I can't?" or "It's your fault!"), sadness (for the thought of needing to give up his/her love affair with the chemical, the people and places he/she use to hang around and the memory of the "good times"), and acceptance to the truth that the chemically dependent person's loss is actually the giving up of their personal hell.

The family members also grieve. We grieve the loss of a fantasy. The fantasy is a relationship we can never have, at least the way we imagine it to be. We are distressed by the bargaining and manipulation we have done to try and save the fantasy. We lament that we have been angry with what we do not understand and have taken it out on our chemically dependent loved ones. We are angry with ourselves because we have not taken care of ourselves. We feel grief for our denial of the part we have played in the affliction. We feel deep sorrow for our denial of how we have been afflicted.

It's not that your relationship did not work.
It's that you gave it goals that were not yours to give

The Role of Acceptance

Acceptance allows you to recognize that right now you are where you need to be. It gives you the patience you need to work on your journey. It helps you understand that another person's work on his or her journey is not your job to figure out. It gives you the wisdom to see that the future of your relationships is not yours to decide. Acceptance shows you that your relationships can never be as they were. It reveals that relationships can be better if you get out of the way. Acceptance means you understand that control is out of your hands. Lastly, acceptance helps you realize that you became involved with a power larger than your understanding. Here lie the seeds of forgiveness.

Acceptance understands the last of the three "C's": "You cannot **cure** it!" It is not up to us to "fix" chemically dependent people. They have to want it more than anything else this world can offer. It really is up to them.

Integrity

Accepting the truth helps us to once again make choices of integrity. Changing the way we interact with chemically dependent people not only brings integrity back into our lives, it also helps those who are chemically dependent. Remember, without personal integrity we are of no help to anyone, especially ourselves.

Integrity means our enabling behaviors are out. We no longer lie for our chemically dependent loved ones, keep secrets for them, tolerate irresponsible behaviors, and avoid the obvious. We no longer argue with them, because the conflict is beyond trying to change their minds with words. We have used words before, only to be involved in endless debate. Our actions must go beyond striking bargains of false hope, because in the past we have not been true to our words on contracts, bargains and threats. Integrity starts with following through on what we say. We refrain from making statements on which we have doubts about our ability to follow through.

The help of Al-Anon for family support becomes important in helping you through your doubts or fears of what might happen if you remain true to your word. You not only have a right, but, more importantly, you also have an obligation to both yourself and your chemically dependent loved one to be true to your word.

Changing your behavior is a process. It is not another manipulative maneuver to try and get chemically dependent people to understand. Trying to get them to understand is a slippery slope of argumentation. What justification will chemically dependent people understand when they are preoccupied with satiating a power greater than both you and themselves?

Trusting the process is being true to your effort.
Knowledge of the outcome is not yours to possess.

If our efforts are aimed at changing chemically dependent people, we will again slip down the slope of trying to out-manipulate master manipulators.

However, it is not so much that they are masters at manipulation as much as it is that they are enslaved to a power greater than themselves. So even though they may fool you or think they are fooling you, it is only because they have fooled themselves first.

Boundaries of Integrity

Boundaries of integrity are changes we make in our interactions with chemically dependent people *that change our lives*. We may not see immediate effects of interruption in the chemically dependent person's lifestyle (the dropping of a pebble in a calm lake does have a ripple effect with ends we cannot always see), but that is not our primary concern, lest we again become involved in trying to manipulate outcomes that do not belong to us.

This next section will allow us to examine how our actions can have an effect on *interrupting* a person's drug-using lifestyle, rather than enabling it, and how to overcome our objections and concerns regarding these actions.

Call the police.

"But the police don't do anything."

You will at least be getting the paper trail started.

Allow them to sit in jail. Allow them to figure out their own bail.

"But this will interrupt their lifestyle."

Exactly.

"But they will learn how to be a criminal!"

They already have.

Don't pay their bills.

"But they don't have enough money to pay them on their own."

Every bill you pay allows them to invest the money they do have in their chemical-using lifestyle.

Allow them to go bankrupt.

"But they will have bad credit."

There is nothing that an honest job won't solve. You can't give it to them if they are not invested in making it work. Allowing them to start over from scratch is the ideal. It really is a total lifestyle change!

Don't drive them around.

"But I need to get them to an AA/NA meeting so they can stay sober."

You can't keep them sober. They have to be the ones who want sobriety more than anything else. If they are resourceful enough to go through enormous lengths to get their chemicals, they can figure out how to get to their AA/NA meetings. Think about it. They will figuratively walk miles, barefoot in a snowstorm, uphill both ways, to get their fix, but they can't go to the meeting around the corner because it's drizzling?

Don't have conversations with them when they have been drinking or are high.

"But I will lose my connection with them."

What connection? Their drug rules.

"But I might be able to give them helpful advice."

What advice of yours has interrupted their chemical use in the past? You don't have the magic solution for them. While they may seem more open to telling you their problems while they are drunk or high, they tell you the same problems over and over again and nothing changes. Don't let your fear deceive you into thinking that this is some kind of special connection you have with them. It's just their drug talking, their way of avoiding the fact that their use is their primary problem, no matter what they talk about.

Speak your truth; don't beat around the bush.

"But I want to make sure they get what I am saying."

They've already turned you off. They are numb to your words. Therefore, say it once, and then move on. Anything more than this makes you a nag. Chemically dependent people lack balance in their lives. We also lack the wisdom of balance.

Don't allow them to live in your home.

"But they might end up living under a bridge, or get taken advantage by someone."

You fear the guilt of them dying out there when you might have been able to save them? They will die more easily with an overdose under your roof because nothing interrupted them. So you are damned if you do and damned if you don't. This is not about you kicking them out. It is about them choosing not to live there because they do not agree to follow the rules of your house. It is about you deciding not to participate in their addiction. Their insanity will not reign in your home unless you invite it in. And if you invite the addiction into your home with the idea of saving them, all you do is invite danger into your home.

"But they threaten to go live with their using friends or drug dealer."

If you give into this threat, your fear of their addiction rules your home and you are its hostage. Though we may try to compromise with the addiction, there is no compromise. The addiction wants it all. Support them by helping speed up the process. Let them live somewhere else. Their consequences are the most sobering thing you can allow. How long will it be until their threat unravels because they don't have money to pay rent or drugs to share with their using friends? Give them the opportunity to burn those bridges. We can let them go, because they are already gone.

Counting the Cost

You do not have to "kick the bum out!" Denying them shelter in your home is about counting the cost. Spouses, are you willing to compromise, to share your relationship with a powerful preoccupation? Are you willing to adjust your relationship with your chemically dependent loved ones by accepting you will not always have intimacy with them? Are you willing to compromise your social life by being embarrassed in public, by having a social life separate from them, and or by staying at home with them, alone, as they use? Are you willing to watch them 'check out' in your presence? Are you willing to parent them, pick up after them? Are you willing to be a single parent?

Be honest. Because if you say you are willing to compromise with their preoccupation and don't accept the truth of your situation, you will be resentful and punish them for it. It is you who chooses to make yourself miserable, not them.

Beyond Belief

Why have we been taken into believing them so many times? Because chemically dependent people have moments of remorse and sincere desire to change. I am not saying that chemically dependent people do not lie and manipulate. They do. But because they have moments of sincere desire to change, we become easily taken into believing them. But then, a moment later, they are chasing after the dealer. "What is going on?!" you ask in confusion and anger. Either you were lied to again or their addiction is more powerful than they are willing to admit. This is not a justification for their behavior. It is an acknowledgment of their willingness to bargain with a cunning, baffling and powerful preoccupation that is always patiently waiting.

Whether or not we should believe them is irrelevant. They have trained us to be suspicious. So be suspicious. But don't be a detective. It is about them demonstrating changed behavior over time. It is not up to you to make sure they follow through.

Interruptions as True Support

Interruptions do not mean chemically dependent people will stop using drugs, but it does mean their lifestyle begins to cost them what they have taken for granted (partially due to our attempts to protect them from pain).

Change occurs when the pain exceeds the pleasure.

There is a price for their addiction. Stop trying to protect them from the price that is theirs to pay; it only delays the process. Interruptions are the teachers that tell them they have a problem and that they need help to stop something they cannot control. Our fearful reactions to protect them from their consequences have helped prolong the process. Experiencing the consequences of their choice to use drugs speeds up this process.

Interruption of their lifestyle allows for hope. But remember, whatever it is we do, the outcome is not ours to choose. Our honesty admits that our actions are no longer based on trying to change our chemically dependent loved ones. We want to change the way we interact with them without the temptation to try and control the outcome. It is for us to "be the change we wish to see in the world." The outcome belongs to God.

Exercise:

Identify and list behaviors (of your own) that you can change that do not have a motive of trying to change (that is, out-manipulate) your chemically dependent loved one. Practice them. Need help? Look back to the section on "What is Support?" and "Boundaries of Integrity" in this chapter, "The Issue of Setting Boundaries" in Chapter Three, or even "Justified Support" in Chapter One to help identify your own enabling actions.

Chapter 5

Healing the Wound

Healing the Wound

Because the body dies, healing involves a goal that unifies the mind.

Peace of mind is that unifying goal.

Resistance

In their attempts to emotionally distance themselves from chemically dependent loved ones, family members often say: "So and so needs to do this or that themselves." My response is, "No, they don't. They don't *need* to do anything!" Again, whatever it is you think the chemically dependent person needs to do is irrelevant to what *you* need to do. Why? Because you're not in control of what he or she will or will not do.

We have resisted the idea that we have been powerless over another person's life. Through this resistance, our lives became unmanageable. Through this unmanageability, we have invited insanity into our lives. This insanity is a preoccupation of anger, abuse, stress, worry, sleepless nights, panic responses at the ring of a phone, poor work ethics, an isolation that affects our relationships, a cynicism about life that affects our ability to play and laugh. We have had to lock our own bedroom doors and the doors of others in our own homes. We have slept with our prized possessions under our pillows. We are afraid to go on vacations for fear of what might happen at home while we are gone. In short, we are hostages in our own homes.

Being the Judge

Relying on a power greater than ourselves to restore us to sanity means we stop being the judge of what the outcome should be. We also stop being the judge of what life situations should mean. Our judgments have given us angry, fearful and guilt-provoking interpretations to our insane encounters with our chemically dependent loved ones. And when we act as the judge, we make God irrelevant to our lives. (Who needs God when I sit on the throne?) Would you like to give up anger, guilt and fear? Then start recognizing that:

It is not your role to judge.

You have judged your past with anger and guilt. This shows that you do not know how to interpret your past. You look into the future as if you have a crystal ball, and all you see are fearfully vague possibilities.

You have been wrong. Be glad, because there is another path to peace of mind. It is not a path of your making, but it does involve your participation. Part of your participation is getting out of the way so you can be shown the path back.

God,
Please let me set aside
everything I think I know
about sobriety, life and You
so I may be open to a new experience. [7]
Amen

Just a Little Willingness

There is freedom in the realization that you do not have to know everything. Actually, you do not have to know *any*thing. Be open to a "still, small voice" giving you direction. You say you do not have a still, small voice? Oh, yes, you do. You just can't hear it above all the other noises and distractions you choose to accept into your mind. Your still, small voice will not compete with your decided agenda. It just waits patiently for your attention.

All you need to do is pray for direction in the midst of your storm. You are not being asked to ignore the distractions. You are being asked for just a little willingness to be redirected in the midst of your conflict.

God does not calm the storm.
He calms His children.

You might feel conflicted, but through your "little willingness," God will supply whatever you perceive you lack. It may not, probably will not, be the way you would have chosen, or according to your timetable or agenda. Still, your willingness to change will start a chain of mighty events for your life. If it comforts you, pray to place your loved ones in God's hands. But rest assured, your loved ones are already in God's hands. So pray instead to recognize reminders that you are also in God's hands.

When you can recognize you already are in God's hands, you will know your loved ones are also.

Opportunity Knocks

The Big Book of Alcoholics Anonymous describes resentment as the "'number one' offender."[8] It explains: "...this business of resentment is infinitely grave. We found that it is fatal. For when harboring such feelings we shut ourselves off from the sunlight of the Spirit. The insanity of alcohol returns and we drink again. And with us, to drink is to die." [9]

The Big Book asks: "How could we escape?"[10] The answer: "We were prepared to look at it from an entirely different angle.... This was our course: We realized that the people who wronged us were perhaps spiritually sick. Though we did not like their symptoms and the way these disturbed us, they, like ourselves, were sick too. We asked God to help us show them the same tolerance, pity, and patience that we would cheerfully grant a sick friend."[11]

Why can we forgive chemically dependent people their insanity? Because "they, like ourselves, were sick too." Chemically dependent people did not see the outcome their preoccupation would bring them. It is cunning. They got sucked in. So did we. It is baffling. Chemically dependent people do not understand it. Do you understand it? It is powerful. Chemically dependent people cannot control their use once they have started. You couldn't keep them from using. That's not because you failed them in any way. It's because it is more powerful than you.

It is your denial that looks upon a cunning, baffling and powerful preoccupation and decides it is "something else." We assume all kinds of reasons, except the real one, for why our chemically dependent loved ones abandon us, abuse us, lie to us, manipulate us, and take advantage of our attempts to help. They really are held captive by a cunning, baffling, powerful preoccupation that is patiently waiting to take them every chance it can. Remember, they deceive us because they deceive themselves first. I'm not trying to give chemically dependent people an excuse for what they have done. Nor do we want to deceive ourselves from seeing our part. The result of our misperception has been anger, hurt and guilt. What you fearfully mistook for "something else" is actually another's insanity, and nothing more. Remember, you also got sucked in and didn't see it coming. When you recognize that your reactions have been adjustments that reflect the chemically dependent person's insanity, you will find the motivation to detach with love. You can experience the miracle of release.

All you are being asked to do is question your judgment of an insanity that can never make sense.

In order to change, you must understand that whatever you perceived your chemically dependent loved ones did to you, was not about you. It was about them, about how they were dealing with their addictions. What they perceived as threat (through their impaired distortions), they took personally and acted out on you. Why you? Because you were the one who was there. This was their way of trying to resolve conflict in their lives. This isn't justification for their behavior; it's clarification.

You, too, err in what you perceive as threat and take personally. Making their error real to you becomes your insanity. Their insanity is not about you—*unless you make it so*. In short, your insanity is not their fault, just like their insanity is not your fault. Again, you are merely being asked to detach from what is not yours and to let go of what you already do not have.

Opportunity knocks—your freedom is at hand!

One of the strongest messages regarding the road to forgiveness comes from Jesus Christ. He was misunderstood, belittled, tortured and crucified for wrongs he did not commit. If any man could feel "justified in anger," it would be him. "Father, send down fire from the sky to consume the unrighteous bastards!" Oh, wait; he didn't say that, did he?

While on the cross, looking at his accusers and executioners, he said, "Father, forgive them for they know not what they do." Not only was he talking about those who looked up at him, he was also talking about us. Jesus saw the way through fear and therefore walked it. When we can understand without exception that others act out their ignorance just like we do, we walk the road of forgiveness to our destination: peace of mind.

The Fellowship

Every day we are granted the opportunity to break the cycle by accepting the miracle of forgiveness. This does not mean we place ourselves once again in harm's way. But it does mean that the road to forgiving our errors leads through forgiving our chemically dependent loved ones, just as the road to forgiving the errors of our chemically dependent loved ones leads through forgiving ourselves.

If you have no concept of a Higher Power, the consciousness of the fellowship you attend will suffice. The binding of any fellowship to a goal towards mutual healing/peace of mind empowers each of us to rise above our misperceptions together, through the contribution of each individual part. This collective consciousness can be a Higher Power for any one who struggles with a personal concept of a Higher Power. And for those who follow the Christian teachings, remember Jesus' promise: "For where two or three have gathered together in my name, there I am in their midst."[12]

Picture yourself with a black rock in your hand. Let's say that the black rock represents your life.

Looking at the rock, you see in it anger, worry and guilt. Not wanting to deal with this rock (that you perceive to be yourself), you might be thinking about hiding it from everyone's view. Or, you might be contemplating the idea of throwing it away. Then a thought enters your mind. This thought slips past your conviction to get rid of the rock. The thought tells you to "place the rock down in front of you, and then step back." You lay the rock down in a place seemingly provided and step back. As you step back, your view of this little black rock opens up into a surprising mosaic. Your little black rock is one of many other black rocks that together form a backdrop. Against this backdrop shines an array of stars. You realize that without the black backdrop, no one would ever see the stars' entire splendor.

The miracle reminds us that it is not we who decide meaning or purpose; our meaning or purpose is determined by our place in a bigger picture. And in that picture is every problem—solved. [13]

Because the whole is greater than the sum of its parts, be that part that trusts the direction of the whole.

Detachment with Love

As we walk into the light of honest recognition, we enter into the arena of different choices. With clarity of the bigger picture comes direction. With the understanding of what our working assumptions and illusions have been, we become free to move towards detachment with love.

Detachment with love is not apathetic indifference, but it also keeps us from feeling forced to do anything. Detachment with love gives us the ability to respond to any situation with a clear purpose. Detachment with love means we do not judge our past mistakes or fear how we might make mistakes in the future. It allows us to understand that we are on a life journey to learn lessons to love again. It helps us understand that our perceived mistakes are a necessary part of the process. This step of faith is beyond our little agenda of control.

What we perceive as mistakes is merely God's way of saying "You are going in the wrong direction. Choose again."

Detachment with love is not about cutting off relationships. Nor is it about judging or trying to change the chemically dependent loved one. It is about setting boundaries between you and the afflicted person. Remember, you cannot control him or her, nor should you want to. Nor should you be involved in trying to convince him or her that what you are doing is the right thing to do. This just leads to further argumentation. Any step of faith is beyond the justification of words. Now you can respond out of your center, a center that is greater than the both of you. You can respond with an empathy that allows your loved one the right to learn from his or her own mistakes.

Who is responsible for your peace of mind? "I am," you say. "Not them?" I ask. "No," you say. Who is responsible for your chemically dependent loved one's peace of mind? "They are," you say. "Not you?" I ask. "No, them," you say. Then get out of the way so they can figure it out! We owe our loved ones this respect. Likewise, we owe ourselves the same respect for learning from our own mistakes, no matter how hard someone else tries to interfere in the name of "support."

A man who carries a cat by the tail learns some-thing he can learn in no other way.

Mark Twain

Integrity recognizes that their journey is theirs, not yours. The lessons they need to learn are theirs. Just as the lessons you need to learn are yours. Although your struggle with them has been a lesson for you, you recognize that this does not justify becoming enmeshed in their problems. Even when you think you know what their problem is, you acknowledge that it is not your problem or your responsibility to solve it. Now you know that you have been wrong about how to solve the problem, and you are grateful that you were wrong, because your way did not work. Now, you are open to another way.

For further work in this area, consider asking yourself these questions.

What blocks your growth to peace of mind? Is it:

- allowing fear to direct your decisions when you know the truth of how things work?
- reliving the past through thoughts of guilt?
- dramatizing situations that are solvable without drama?
- holding onto fragments of your life because you can't think of a way to exist without them, even though you know they are self-defeating?
- lacking faith in your inner guide for direction?

What will assist your journey to peace of mind? Is it:

- trusting your inner guide for direction?
- identifying and interrupting thoughts of worry

about the future with an understanding that all is well?

- identifying and interrupting thoughts of guilt about the past with an understanding that you are forgiven?

- releasing beliefs and judgments from your life that at one time seemed "sacred," but that now you can live without?

- meditation and prayer that includes celebrating everything in your life with gratitude and asking continually, "What is it You want me to know?" instead of trying to guess what might be the solution to the problem at hand?

- accepting that peace with your loved one's chemical dependency will only come when your goal in everything you think, do and say is peace of mind?

Exercise:

Without exception, put all your thoughts of the past (fond memories, guilt, resentment, etc.) aside. Again without exception, put all your thoughts of the future (anticipation, anxiety, fear, etc.) aside. Lastly, put aside all discomforts and distractions of your physical body. What problem do you have in this present moment? Only list the thoughts that have nothing to do with the past, future, and bodily distractions.

When you have worked through this process of elimination in your mind, you will realize the answer to the question "What problem do you have in this present moment?" is: "Nothing."

Any present moment in which you choose to be beyond mind and body will be a place of peace. There is no past or future. There never has been. Because there is no agenda of your own that gets in the way, you cultivate a place where you can once again remember your real relationship with God and one another.

When you leave this place, you will again take up your worries and cares. But this place of peace will always be with you, waiting for you when you again choose to want it more than anything else. And every time you come back to this place, the door will open a little wider, until this place of peace is the only place you want.

Something to Think About

I asked for strength . . .
And God gave me difficulties to make me strong.

I asked for wisdom . . .
And God gave me problems to solve.

I asked for prosperity . . .
And God gave me a brain and brawn to work.

I asked for courage . . .
And God gave me danger to overcome.

I asked for love . . .
And God gave me troubled people to help.

I asked for favors . . .
And God gave me opportunities.

I received nothing I wanted.
I received everything I needed.

Anonymous

Footnote references:

[1] **An alternative ending to our opening story**
With total exhaustion and much sorrow, the fox finally let the scorpion go. Immediately, he felt lighter in the water and able to see the other side. He had not realized that through the direction of the scorpion, he had been swimming in circles, and usually against the current. But now, with clarity, he could see the direction he needed to go.

[2] The name "God" is one name among many other names across different cultures and languages. This name of many names is universally recognized as the all-knowing source of our being, and we participate in this source as its children. This relationship to our source makes us all brother's and sister's. I will be using the name "God" and "Higher Power" interchangeably.

[3] Alcoholics Anonymous, pp. 58-59.

[4] McLellan AT, Lewis DC, O'Brien CP, and Kleber HD. Drug dependence, a chronic medical illness: Implications for treatment, insurance, and outcomes evaluation. JAMA 284(13): 1689-1695, 2000.

[5] Alcoholics Anonymous, p. 58.

[6] From *Courage to Change—One Day at a Time in AlAnon II*, copyright 1992, by AlAnon Family Group Headquarters, Inc. Reprinted by permission of AlAnon Family Group Headquarters, Inc., p. 208.

[7] Anonymous.

[8] Alcoholic Anonymous, p. 64.

[9] Ibid., p. 66.

[10] Ibid., p. 66.

[11] Ibid., pp. 66-67.

[12] Matthew 18:20, New American Standard Version of the Bible.

[13] Not only is every problem in the picture, but the problem exists simultaneously as one that has already been solved. God's vision is eternal—outside the illusion of time.

Quick Order Form

Postal Orders: Please send check or money order to:

Karayan Publishing
PO Box 366,
Buffalo, MN 55313

Price: $15.00 per book
MN sales tax: 0.97 per book (6.5%)
Shipping: 3.00 for first book and
                 2.00 for each additional book

Total: **$18.97 for first book**

Name: _____

Address: _____

City: _____ State: _____ Zip: _____

Telephone: _____

Email Address: _____

Please send information on:

❏ Other Books   ❏ Speaking/Seminars   ❏ Consulting